How to get the best out of your

of your

Freezer

Marianne Duvall.

ISBN: 9798644252985

Contents

Introduction

If you've read any of my books, you'll probably have noticed that the freezer is one of my favourite pieces of kitchen equipment.

Most of us have a freezer, even if it's just a small section above the fridge, but so many freezers are just another cupboard for ready meals from the store, packets or trays of ice and tubs of ice cream.

But it can be much more useful than that.

A freezer can help you to embrace a healthy lifestyle.

- A freezer can save you money.
- A freezer can save you time.
- A freezer can allow you to make the most of fruit and vegetables when they're in season.

- A freezer can stop you wasting food.
- A freezer can save your herbs.
- A freezer can help you make the most of your garden produce.
- A freezer is amazing.

In this book, I want to show you how to truly embrace your freezer. How to make it a central part of your food preparation and storage.

How it can help you to be healthier, save money and be more environmentally aware.

As we begin this second decade of the 21st-century, we have all had to stop and re-evaluate our relationship with food. Dealing with coronavirus has shown us that it's not always possible to pop to the local restaurant or takeaway.

It hasn't even been possible to pop into the shops every day.

It's made us realise that it's much more important to think about our food supplies than we were used to.

We can't survive without food and we've become too used to a constant, never ending stream of food.

But this is also meant that we have become huge wasters of food.

We buy too much, let it go off and then throw it away.

Some studies have shown that in America, almost 60% of the food that households buy ends up being thrown away.

That can cost more than the heating bill, property taxes or gas. And some studies put the figures for the UK even higher.

That's not good for your pocket, it's not good for your health, and it's certainly not good for the environment.

In fact, not only is it an enormous waste of money, it's horrifying to think of that much food being wasted when people are going hungry.

A lot of waste is due to food going off, no one really wants to eat furry fruit or green bread, but there's also a huge amount of food that is thrown away because people 'fear' that it has gone off.

Best before dates are really a guide not a fixed limit, with most food, you can tell if it's still okay to eat or not – that tell-tale furry coat or green spots.

There are some foods that you do have to take more care with, but they are marked with 'Use By' dates rather than 'best before' dates, they are for foods that can cause problems rather than just tasting or looking unpleasant, and you should take note of those dates

But when you embrace your freezer as more than a cupboard for ready meals, ice cream and pizza, you will develop a completely different outlook on your food supply, and you'll wonder how you ever managed before.

The idea of throwing away good food will become an anathema to you.

You'll discover how much money you can save by using the food you bring into the house, and you'll get tastier, healthier food for you and your family.

You'll learn to portion and freeze food that you know you're not going to use in time. You'll also learn to label it with what it is and – very important – what date you actually put it into the freezer, so you will always know when you have to use it by.

Saving 60% or more of your food budget is an excellent reason to learn to embrace your freezer.

Being able to enjoy tastier, healthier food is another even better reason.

Understanding Frozen

We seem to have developed an idea that frozen food is somehow second-rate food, nothing could be further from the truth. Take the example of the humble pea.

If you go and buy fresh peas in their pods from the shops or in the greengrocers, you are buying them as fresh peas still in their pods, to take home and go through the ritual of shelling them.

That means they're really fresh, doesn't it?

Actually, no it doesn't.

Unless you buy them from a stall at the edge of the field, or go and pick them from your garden or allotment, they're really not that fresh.

They have been picked, then they've been packed, then they been put on a lorry, then they've been moved probably to a wholesaler, then they been bought, then they've been moved again to the shop, then you arrived at the shop and chosen them and taken them home.

That journey, even if it has happened quite locally, has taken a few days. And it might actually have taken those humble peas across a few countries and they might have been chilled to hold them in a kind of suspended animation for their journey.

Now think of the frozen pea, that poor relation.

They have been picked, taken to the factory, frozen.

This can happen in just a few hours. And once they are frozen they stay at that level of freshness, so although they are then packed and transported and moved again to the shops and put in the freezers before you go and buy them and take them to your freezer, you are still buying them as if they had just been picked. Two hours ago.

You will read in some places that fruit and vegetables lose some of their nutrients when they are frozen, but studies have shown that this just isn't the case.

Fresh produce begins to lose some of the nutrients as soon as it is picked. Those fresh peas can lose up to half their vitamin C in the first 24 hours.

Studies comparing fresh and frozen fruit and vegetables have shown that there is no real difference between them, with some frozen.

And this story can be repeated across all types of frozen vegetables.

So buying frozen is really the next best thing to going and picking them yourself and cooking them straight away.

And there is another benefit to having frozen vegetables.

It means that when you are putting some peas or leeks or cauliflower into your casserole, you only use the amount you need for that recipe. The rest stays in the packet in the freezer.

Compare that to using fresh where you only use the amount you need, put the rest back in the fridge, forget about it for a few days, taken out the fridge and put in the bin.

So you have very fresh produce, no washing, preparing and chopping and no waste.

Added to that the fact that frozen vegetables are often much cheaper than fresh vegetables and the choice becomes obvious.

Frozen vegetables aren't second-rate at all, apart from going and picking my own from the vegetable patch, frozen vegetables are one of my favourites.

It doesn't stop at veggies.

If you are not a vegetarian, (I am) check out frozen meat and fish. As long as it is still good quality, sustainable – and if I ate meat I would always choose free range and organic – then frozen will often save you money, and if you are cooking a curry, pie filling or casserole, you probably won't even notice a difference, except to your wallet.

Freezer Safety

Making sure your food is safe should always be top of the list in the list of reasons for using a freezer.

Convenience is great, saving money is wonderful, reducing food waste and doing your bit for the environment is always a good aim, but keeping you safe from food poisoning really is top of the list.

There are a few things that are really important if you want your food to stay safe in the freezer.

Junk in, junk out

This used to be a popular phrase in computing and it's just as relevant here.

Always start with good and preferably fresh food.

Yes, it is possible to freeze food that is getting close to its use date when you know you won't use it, it's better than throwing it out.

But when you defrost it, it will still be close to its use by date. If it's beginning to go mushy when you freeze it, it will still be past its best when you defrost it.

So get into the habit of thinking of the freezer as a way of keeping food in the best condition rather than just preventing wastage.

Temperature.

Keeping the temperature of your freezer and your fridge at a safe operating level will mean that they both work better. The food stays safer and you save money by using them as efficiently as possible

You can pick up a set of two thermometers easily for less than the cost of a good dinner out.

Check your temperature.

Freezer burn

Freezer burn happens, but it's better to avoid it.

It can discolour your meat or cover your food with small ice crystals.

The food is still absolutely safe to eat, but freezer burn can change the texture or the taste as well as the look of your food, so it's much better to avoid it if you can.

Freezer burn is caused by freezing air.

It is the effect of dehydration when frozen food is exposed to air. So it's important to keep the air out.

Wrapping food really well is the main way to avoid freezer burn.

If there isn't any air, there isn't any freezer burn.

If you are using freezer bags, try to push all of the air out before you seal it. If you are using freezer containers, wrap the food tightly in freezer and food safe wrap before putting it in the box.

If you are making things like soups, sauces and casseroles for the freezer, cool them before freezing so that you don't warm any other food it might be sitting next to.

Don't keep opening the freezer. Each time you open the door you are allowing warm air in. Having your freezer well organised will make it easier to find and get what you are looking for quickly.

If you are doing a lot of freezing, it's worth considering investing in a vacuum sealer. It might seem like just another gadget, but if you intend to use your freezer to help with budgeting and storing food you will get good use out of it. By its very nature, it removes all the air from your portions. No air, no freezer burn.

Suitable containers

Not every container is suitable for the freezer.

Don't use glass unless it states that it is safe – glass can crack when frozen. If you do use freezer safe glass, this is the one time you do need to leave space in the container to allow for expansion.

Don't assume any food bag is the same.

You can find many types of food storage bag in the shops.

You can pick up a pack of sandwich bags from any food store but that doesn't make them suitable for the freezer.

Check the label.

Freezer bags are made to withstand freezing.

They are made of thicker, freezer safe plastic which is designed to be able to cope with the extreme temperature. Ordinary bags can become brittle and disintegrate.

Choose resealable freezer bags and containers that are marked as suitable for food and freezer use.

Of course, you could also use that vacuum sealer with approved bags.

Portion size.

Freeze your food in sizes that you will use, whether that is single portion, enough for two or a bigger amount for feeding the family.

This means that it will be easier to choose and use the food from the freezer.

You will be able to find the meal you want or the ingredients you need for a recipe without having to empty half the freezer.

You will be able to take out the amount you want to use, and it will thaw out faster, ready for use.

Remember, you cannot re-freeze food once you have thawed it out.

So if you are buying or picking in bulk, or batch cooking, don't freeze in bulk.

Thawing

You can use some foods straight from the freezer.

Frozen berries into a smoothie or mixed with yoghurt to create a flavoured treat.

Frozen peas into a pasta at the last minute or frozen flavour bombs into a sauce or casserole.

And of course, suitable frozen meals straight into the microwave and on your plate in under ten minutes.

If you plan on doing this, don't store them in aluminium trays.

But most foods, and especially any high protein food like meat, has to be thawed properly to make sure it's safe to eat.

Take it from the freezer and place it in the fridge overnight.

The larger the item you are thawing, the longer it will take.

Do not leave it on the counter.

This can expose the food to bacteria and contamination that will make it unsafe to eat and in a worse case, can cause food poisoning.

Some prepacked meat and fish products such as burgers, chicken goujons or fish fingers are designed to be cooked from frozen, but always check the packaging and if in any doubt, or if you have frozen the food yourself, allow it to thaw slowly and safely in the refrigerator.

Start by Organising

If you want to make the most of your freezer, it's really important to organise it.

I'm sure we've all faced the time when we find ourselves falling into the base of a chest freezer or digging out the back of the drawers in an upright freezer, and finding foods that have been there since - well, who knows when?

That is not the best way to make the most of your freezer.

So it is important to organise it rather than just opening it and dropping stuff in.

What do you want from your freezer?

And it's important when you are planning the organisation of your freezer, that you know what you want from it.

Do you just use it to store frozen pizzas and ice cream? Or do you batch cook and store your own ready meals?

There's no point spending money buying a whole load of special containers and freezer bags, if all you ever do is go to the supermarket and fill it up with ready packed items. Although it can be worth it if you plan to buy big and store small.

You've probably already got a freezer, but if you're planning on replacing it or you're setting up a new home, it's worthwhile spending some time to decide what you really want to use it for.

A couple of years ago, I replaced the chest freezer that I had in the garage with an upright freezer with drawers.

The reason?

I got sick of falling into the chest freezer when I was trying to reach something at the bottom!

I also found it much too easy to discover that the food was at that was at the bottom of the pile had been there for a number of years rather than months.

You can also decide between a large upright freezer, mine is 6 foot tall, with six drawers, or if space is at a premium, you can have a fridge freezer.

As a personal choice, in a fridge freezer, I prefer the freezer part of that to be on the bottom, simply because I find that if the fridge is on the bottom, I put things in the fridge, don't see them when I open the door and then forget what's there.

Whereas if I open the door and look straight in at eye level, I am always aware of what fresh goods are available. And for me, having the fridge at eye level rather than the freezer is more important, because the fridge is opened much more regularly than the freezer.

It's just personal choice, but it's worth thinking about before you spend your money.

Another point to remember is that if you are planning on having your freezer in the garage or an outhouse, many brands will not cover it and the guarantee won't be valid. Being outside the main home means it can get too cold.

Whoever realised a freezer could be too cold?

This might sound strange, but it's very important if you have to use the guarantee or your insurance, and of course you want the freezer to work as efficiently as it is intended to.

So, if you are planning on keeping your freezer outside the main part of the home, check that it will be covered.

Sorting before changing

If you are starting with your existing freezer, and most of us are, take the time to sort out the food you have before you think about any changes.

If you look in your freezer and find that there are bags of healthy beans, that have been there for longer than you care to remember, then you probably aren't going to use them.

Good intentions are fine, but it's what you actually use that matters.

So if you find that you do have an overabundance of a certain type of food, there's really no point in buying any more.

You might find that it's full of pizzas and frozen ready meals that are used and replaced on a reg ular basis.

If that is what you choose - and why not, if it suits your lifestyle - then it's important to find a freezer that will match your decisions.

It's also important to de-clutter.

Get rid of the items that have been there far too long, clean the freezer out and then reorganise it.

Knowing what you want from your machine is really important before you can decide how best to use it.

What can you freeze?

If you're going to make the most of your freezer, it's also important to know what you can freeze.

I've covered this in another part of the book, but it's important at this stage to realise that some things can be frozen and some things can't.

Don't just assume that you can freeze anything you bring home from the store.

Check the information on the packaging.

Some items have been pre-frozen in transport and it's important never to re-freeze food

It's also important to realise that the length of time you can leave something in a freezer, does vary.

And if you do your own batch cooking and store items in odd containers and freezer bags, you really do need to know what is in them, and when you froze them.

Check the temperature

It's also important to make sure that you've got the temperature of your freezer right.

A freezer thermometer is easy to find and won't cost you very much but it can save you quite a lot of money.

Very often the freezer is not working as efficiently as it could.

Ideally, a freezer should be running at about -18 ° Centigrade which is 0 ° Fahrenheit. A thermometer will help you check that you are keeping it at the right temperature

And try and keep it full.

A half empty freezer is freezing the air in empty spaces. So when you open the door, the air escapes and then the freezer has to work even harder to bring the temperature back down. But if it's full and well packed without too many spaces, there isn't as much air to escape or enough space for warm air to enter.

If you have a powercut – keep the freezer door closed. The frozen food inside it will stay frozen for longer.

When the power comes back on, check the contents. Anything still frozen solid will be fine, anything that has defrosted but is still very cold, will be fine but use it, don't leave it inside to re-freeze.

Anything you're not sure about – get rid of it.

And while we're on the subject of defrosting.

When you take items out of the freezer, put them in the fridge to defrost slowly rather than leaving them on the bench where they could develop bacteria. It's important to be especially careful with meat, poultry and fish.

Keep it clean

If you don't have a machine that automatically defrost itself, and even if you do, you should check it, it's important to defrost and deep clean the freezer.

It's also important to get to the workings on the outside rear of the freezer to make sure that it isn't covered in dust, because this can make it inefficient in operation and can be dangerous.

Part of organising is not only to clean everything out before you start but ensure that you keep it clean and organised.

If anything spills, wipe it up.

If any loose items drop out of bags or boxes, remove them.

If it needs to be defrosted manually, do it regularly and when you are cleaning, don't forget the rubber seals. Most people do forget to clean those frames around the door of the freezer, but it is the area most susceptible to mould, because it is the area where the temperature changes are most extreme

Storage

If you are going to freeze and batch cook sauces, casseroles and soups, it can save a lot of space if you store them in bags rather than boxes.

It means that you can get a lot more in the freezer without wasting the space around the boxes or the space inside the boxes that are not full.

It also means you can keep the portion size right.

Fill your bag with one or two portions, depending on your lifestyle, squeeze out the excess air and then put them in the freezer, laying flat, one on top of the other like a pile of books.

Once they are frozen and labelled, you will be able to stand them upright if you want and it will make it much easier and much more efficient to be able to remove one and use it that day.

Lying food flat as it freezes also avoids creating big lumps of frozen something.

For instance, if you're freezing berries.

If you lie them flat and freeze them in a single layer, you'll not only save space, but you won't have a huge lump of strawberries that are virtually unusable.

An added benefit is that you will be able to open it and take out a handful of the time, rather than removing the whole bag, and drop a couple of them into your smoothies or yoghurt dessert

Using frozen fruit in your smoothies is amazing, because you are getting the ice and the fruit in one go.

Learn to label

Label things as you put them in the freezer.

Label it with what it is and label the date you've put it there.

When you are re-organising your freezer, it's a good time to check what you actually do, rather than what you'd like to be doing. Reality and imagination are not always the same thing.

Is the freezer fully of 'healthy' food that you plan to eat but always bypass as you reach for a pizza?

If you discover that you have lots of cartons of carrot and orange soup that have been there for too long, it's a good guess that you don't actually like carrot and orange soup.

It seems like a good idea when you make it, but then you never choose it when you're deciding on what to eat that evening.

So be honest with yourself and get rid of the food that you haven't and won't eat, and plan on making a new start.

This book isn't about creating a new healthier lifestyle, although that's always a good idea. But this book is about living your life more efficiently in regards to your freezer.

If you decide to make healthier choices, eat more fruit and veg and embrace home cooking along the way, that's great.

But we're concentrating on getting more out of your freezer at the moment, in reality.

Again - Learn to Label

So what is in that strange green stuff in the bag at the very bottom of the drawer?

The only way to identify it is to label it.

Is it parsley? Is it basil? Is it spinach? Sometimes once they are frozen, you really can't tell.

Is that red sauce beetroot, red cabbage or a berry mix. You don't want to find out by pouring beetroot soup all over your chocolate cake.

So learning to label your produce is a vital way of getting the best out of your freezer. Because if you don't label it, you look at it, wonder what it is and end up throwing it away.

It also means that you will be able to keep your foods safe.

For instance, some foods are perfectly safe for up to a year, whereas others should really only be kept for two or three months

Buying in Bulk

You can save a lot of money by buying in bulk rather than in the normal smaller family size packaging.

However, this can make it a little bit difficult to store and use.

So I always split the bulk purchase into portion sizes that suit me. You can do this either with freezer bags or with containers that are suitable for the freezer.

I particularly like boxes that I can take from the freezer and put straight into the microwave, very useful if you need to save some time. Freezer boxes are also very good for items that are oddly shaped and won't easily sit in a freezer bag.

If you are using containers rather than bags for your freezer, and you want to use them in the microwave, do remember not to use metal ones.

If you are getting really serious about freezing and particularly if you buy in bulk, grow your own or batch cook, then it might be worth thinking about investing in a vacuum sealer.

Using a vacuum sealer to create portion sizes that suit you and your family means that you can save a lot of space in your freezer, you can avoid freezer burn by removing any air in the food, You can easily see what you have stored when you use transparent bags that you have labelled.

It also means that you can avoid the wasted space and the risk of freezer burn that you get when you buy frozen food in cardboard boxes. The food is packed inside the box as well, and although boxes make it easy for the supermarkets to store and display their foods, it can make it bulky when you want to put it in your home freezer. If you are doing this, then write the instructions on your packaging or, I prefer, to simply cut the instructions from the box and stick it to my new packaging.

If your freezer has shelves rather than drawers, don't forget that very often you can adjust the height of the shelves and make the space work for you rather than just accept it the way the manufacturer has set it up.

You can freeze milk. It's very useful to have some emergency milk when you can't get to the shops.

But once you've used the milk from its plastic container you can reuse it. The container, not milk. They are normally quite square and easy to store and you can store fluids or small vegetables such as sweet corn, chopped carrots or frozen peas.

As I said earlier, the reason I replaced my chest freezer for an upright one was because I got sick of falling into the bottom when I was trying to reach stuff.

And the problem with a chest freezer is that when you buy or make new stuff, it is very tempting to simply put it in the top of the food already there. After all, what else are you going to do?

And you use the food from the top unless you specifically want something that you know is at the bottom of the pile.

In practice, this tends to result in the stuff that is at the bottom of the freezer staying there.

And staying there so long that in the end you have to throw it out.

So organising a chest freezer is even more important that organising an upright freezer.

You can get baskets that will fit in a chest freezer or you can use larger storage boxes, which means that you can put all your vegetables in one, all your deserts in another, cooked meals in third, soups in a fourth, and of course, if you are a meat eater, you can have boxes for your meat and for your fish.

That means that you will know where your different types of food are rather than having to empty out the whole thing as you scrabble for that mac and cheese that you know was in there somewhere.

Freezing Fresh Produce

There are many reasons for freezing fresh produce.

You might grow your own, or someone else does and then shares their harvest with you.

You might find a great offer on something at the food store because it is in season.

You might make trips to a farm shop and bulk buy to make the trip worthwhile.

You might not be able to get out to the shops as often as you would like to or live quite a distance from the store.

You might even be in the middle of a global pandemic – but let's hope that doesn't come around again anytime soon.

There are all sorts of reasons that can result in a kitchen counter full of strawberries, or mangos, a large bag of cauliflower or garden peas.

And as you look at your haul, you realise that unless you have carrots for every meal – including breakfast – for the next week, there's just no way you're going to be able to get through them all while they are still fresh.

That's when your freezer can really come into its own and help you to save a small fortune on the grocery bill as well as saving you from food waste.

But a bit of prior knowledge does help.

It helps to know which fruit and vegetable are freezer friendly so you can plan ahead for your trip to the store or farmers market.

And of course, if you are growing your own, it's important to know what you can store and freeze so that you don't waste any of your crop.

Decide what foods you will freeze as ingredients and which ones you will make up into meals first.

Carrots, cauliflower and peas are fine as bags of ready to use ingredients, but I prefer to make aubergine (eggplant) and courgettes (zucchini) into meals and then freeze them.

Of course, it's good to share the glut of the harvest with friends and family, but it's also good to stock up your own food store for later.

A great many fruit and veggies are perfect for the freezer, but not all.

That means that it's useful to know which ones you can get the best out of.

What should be cooked?

What should be stored in other ways?

What should be eaten fresh?

Most fruits can be frozen after being cleaned and possibly chopped, but many vegetables can need some preparation.

Most vegetables will require you to blanch them for about 5 minutes and then dip them into ice water to stop the cooking process before they can be frozen, but we'll go into that later.

Start by choosing fruits and vegetables you plan to freeze at the peak of ripeness.

Remember – junk in, junk out.

If you freeze your food in peak condition, it will still be in good condition when it comes back out again.

If you freeze it when it's getting close to the choice between freezer and bin, it's still going to be close to that choice when it comes back out.

Freezing Fruit

Let's start with fruit.

Whether you're storing your own crop, going to a farmer's market or farm shop, or buying from the local grocer or giant supermarket, you should choose the best fruits you can get.

The food should be firm and without bruises to make sure you still have the best taste when you use them in the future.

Don't be afraid to sniff and feel the fruit to see how fresh it is. You don't want a basket full of bruised and damaged fruit to start with

Frozen lemon or lime slices are a lovely alterative to ice cubes, and cubes of de-seeded watermelon are perfect to give a hint of flavour to a glass of water or to add into your smoothie.

Although you can freeze your fruit when it's fresh and at its best, if you have to you can also freeze it when it's beginning to turn, it's certainly a better option than the bin or the compost heap.

It's quite normal to find that you bought a bunch of bananas, but you didn't eat them all and now they are beginning to go off.

Most people think that means they have to be used in smoothies or in making banana bread, and of course they can, but you can also freeze them.

With bananas, peel it and chop it, with apples, slice them, the same with pears.

If you have plums or mangoes or other stone fruit, take the stone out and cut them into slices or cubes.

The best way to freeze fruit to make it easy-to-use afterwards, is to put it in a single layer on a tray and flash freeze it, or inside a Ziploc bag, something like a sealable freezer bag, any method where they can freeze flat, in a single layer.

Once they are frozen you can store them in whichever way suits you, but freezing them flat means that they won't all descend into a solid lump, and you can simply snap a piece off when you want some fruit.

You can freeze in their individual types, a bag of blueberries, a bag of mango chunks, a bag of apple slices, or you can make your own fruit mix.

Although many fruits have a change in texture as you freeze them, they are still perfect in a smoothie or with some yoghurt, great to make your own ice cream, ideal for making jams or chutneys and can easily be turned into pies and puddings.

If you have got some leftover compote or pie filling, that can be frozen as well. Compotes are one of those things that are perfect in an ice cube tray to make a fruity cooler for your cocktail or to flavour water.

When you are freezing fruit, you have to realise that when it is defrosted, it will never have the same texture as the fresh fruit.

Fresh fruit contains a lot of water, so when you freeze the fruit, the structure of it will change.

That means you probably won't want to take frozen fruit out and put it on your salad or decorate a cake in the way that you would with fresh fruit, but it still perfect for all sorts of other reasons, because the taste is retained.

You can use various ways to treat the fruit before you freeze it.

For instance, a quick dip in lemon juice will help stop browning in things like apples or pears.

Blanching, bringing it to the boil briefly, and then plunging into a bath of icy water, can help preserve the colour and a certain amount of texture in some fruits.

You can freeze the fruit on a baking sheet to keep them separate, and then transfer them into your storage container.

You freeze them until they are firm - anywhere from 30 minutes to 4 hours depending on the fruit - and once they are frozen, just put them in your storage container or freezer bag and they should stay separate instead of being one solid mass.

Most types of fruit they should be fine in your freezer for up to a year, but to keep their flavour as strong as possible, you really should use them after six months maximum.

There are different preparation methods to get the best out of various fruit

Apples

peel, core and slice them, then dip them quickly in lemon juice to preserve the colour and then freeze for up to 6 months.

Apricots.

Blanche the apricots and pat dry. Remove the stones, freeze and store for about three months.

Avocados

Cut the avocado in half, remove the seed and the peel and freeze.

You can also store the avocado as a purée, add a few drops of lime juice to prevent the browning and freeze for up to 3 months.

Bananas

Peel, and slice, or purée, and freeze for up to 6 months.

Blueberries.

Wash and pat dry and freeze for up to 6 months.

Cherries

Wash the cherries remove the stems and stones and freeze for up to 6 months.

Coconut

Drain and save the milk, cut the flesh into cubes or shred it and freeze for up to 6 months.

Cranberries

Wash and dry, freeze for up to 6 months.

Grapes.

Frozen grapes make a lovely and usual fruity treat and are perfect served with cheese, there is no need to defrost them.

Kiwi

Peel and slice a ripe Kiwi, you can also cut it into chunks. It will freeze for up to 6 months.

Lemons and limes.

Slices of lemons or limes will freeze for up to 6 months and are perfect to cool and flavour your drink at the same time.

Mango

Peel the mango and cut it into slices or chunks, it's best to pre-freeze so the pieces stay separated and it will last for up to 6 months.

Melon.

Whichever type of melon you are using, peel it, remove the seeds, cut it into strips or cubes . It will last for up to 6 months.

Oranges.

You can either cut the orange into slices or peel it and separate the sections. The same is true for other types of orange or grapefruit. They will last for up to 6 months.

Papaya

peel it and remove the seeds, cut it into strips or chunks, and it will last for up to 6 months.

Peaches

remove the stone and cut into chunks, and it will last for up to 6 months.

Pears

peel, core and slice, dip briefly into lemon juice to retain the colour and they will freeze for up to 6 months.

Plums

cut them into chunks and remove the stones and they will freeze for up to 6 months.

Pineapple

remove the skin and the core and then freeze as slices or chunks, and they will last for up to 6 months

Pomegranates.

It is the seeds you want to freeze, so this card the rest, freeze them in a single layer, and they will last for up to 6 months.

Berries.

Raspberries, strawberries, blackberries, all sorts of berries can be frozen very easily.

Remove the stems and either leave them whole or cut them into pieces as you prefer, and they will freeze for up to 6 months

If you want to retain some texture, add a little sugar before freezing

Watermelon is mainly water, so it does freeze but it doesn't thaw very well.

I do use it as a flavoured ice cube, although to be honest it doesn't retain much flavour. Try it if you have some watermelon that you're about to throw out and see what you think.

Fruits which freeze well include:

- Apples
- Apricots
- Bananas
- Berries of all kinds
- Cherries
- Coconut
- Cranberries
- Citrus
- Grapes
- Nectarines
- Peaches
- Pears
- Pineapple
- Plums
- Raspberries
- Rhubarb
- Strawberries

Marianne Duvall

Freezing Vegetables

The advice on how to freeze vegetables successfully can sometimes make it sound like a time-consuming task, but it isn't really, so instead of putting it off, once you've gone through this routine, you realise it's quite simple.

Prepare the vegetables into the sizes you want to freeze, chunks or slices are good for most vegetables.

Blanching them involves putting them in boiling water for between 1 and 5 minutes depending on the size and the vegetable, taking them out, dunking them in ice cold water to stop the cooking, taking them out of that and drying them off.

Then lay them flat on a freezer tray, freeze them for a couple of hours, package them in their bags or containers carefully labelled with the details, such as what type of vegetable and the date it was frozen.

But you don't have to go through this process.

Freezing food is a method of preservation that goes way back well before we had things like freezers or even electricity.

Freezing can maintain the natural colour. The flavour and the nutritional value of fresh foods.

The most important rule about freezing vegetables. If you want to maintain the nutrition, is to freeze them as quickly as possible.

As soon as something is picked. It begins to lose some of its nutritional value, that's why frozen peas from the supermarket contained so many more vitamins than fresh peas that have in reality been travelling for days.

As long as you are prepared for your vegetables to have a shorter freezer life, they don't always have to be blanched. If you want to store your fruit and veg for a month or two, simply prepare them, then freeze them

For this short term freezing you can treat them in much the same way as you do fruit.

Just chop them into the sizes you want, make sure they are clean and dry and freeze them.

But if you want your vegetables to last longer in the freezer, a year to 18 months, then it's important to prepare your vegetables first by blanching them.

This might sound a bit of a faff, but it is not, and it is well worth it.

Again, prepare your vegetables into the shapes and sizes that you want, then blanch and shock them.

This means boiling them very briefly, draining them and plunging them into ice water to stop the cooking process. Then dry them thoroughly and freeze them.

Blanching means that your vegetables will maintain their colour and flavour as well as the nutrients. It also keeps them safer by destroying any bacteria or microorganisms that might be on the surface of the vegetables.

Although you can freeze almost anything, some survive the freezing process better than others.

When you are using frozen vegetables they are best used in things like casseroles, soups, curries and stews.

Vegetables and fruits that are used in a salad very often have a high water content, and they don't freeze very well, or at least they defrost in a very mushy way.

So things like cucumbers, lettuce, cabbages, radishes and tomatoes, just aren't going to be the same as their fresh cousins.

On the other hand, vegetables such as corn, peas, broccoli, cauliflower, carrots, green beans, greens such as kale, spinach and chard, and winter squash are very good for freezing.

Onions, peppers and celery also freeze well.

Preparing onions is not one of my favourite jobs, so I prefer to prepare a lot of them, preferably in a food processor, and then freeze them up inconvenient portion size bags.

They're perfect for when you're in a hurry and don't want to start chopping onions, and you can save all your crying for one large batch.

Why and how to blanch.

If you want to get the best out of freezing vegetables, whether you have grown them yourself, bought them from the farm shop or just got a really good deal at the food store, it's important to be able to store your harvest.

Technically, the reason for blanching is that it can stop the action of enzymes that can change the flavour, the colour and the texture of your vegetables.

It cleans the surface of the food from dirt and organisms, it helps slow the loss vitamins, it can brighten the colour and on a practical note, it can also soften vegetables and make them easier to pack and store.

Cooking some vegetables can save a lot of space. The difference in size of raw or cooked and frozen spinach is amazing, and the frozen spinach tastes just them same as cooked from raw. You just wouldn't want to use it on your salad instead of nice fresh leaves.

It's important to get the timing of the blanching right, depending on the vegetable and the size you have prepared it into.

If you blanch it for too long, it's the same as any other way of cooking vegetables for too long.

You lose the flavour.

The colour and flavour leech out into the water and you lose the vitamins and minerals.

On the other hand, if you don't blanch them long enough, you can actually stimulate the activity of the enzymes.

As we are talking about doing this at home and not in a great big factory, blanching means dunking the vegetables in boiling water and then cold or iced water to stop the cooking process.

The blanching time does depend on different vegetables and with all vegetables, the size of the vegetable or the size of the chunks you have cut it into will alter the amount of time it requires, in the same way as it would if you were actually cooking them.

Asparagus

If you are freezing small stalks you should blanch them for about two minutes, whereas large stalks would need four minutes. Fresh crisp asparagus is best of course, if you freeze limp asparagus it will be even worse when it thaws

Beans

Fresh green beans are perfect for freezing. Wash and trim the ends. Prepare them as you prefer to cook them, either slicing length wise or cutting into pieces.

They take between two and four minutes.

You can dry broad beans, but they are also a good choice for freezing.

Pod them, rinse them and blanch them for no longer than 2 minutes

After washing and trimming, blanch runner beans for about 3 minutes.

Broccoli

Cut the broccoli into florets of about 1½ inches, and allow three minutes blanching time. Then freeze flat on a tray to keep the pieces separate. Bag once frozen.

I like to use the stalks and leaves as well. Treat the leaves as other spring greens. Leave the smaller stalks on the florets and slice the thicker stalks into discs, they will keep their crunch.

Brussels sprouts

Brussel sprouts are small cabbages would take between three and five minutes. Take them off the stalk and wash them. When you want to use them, they are best roasted from frozen to avoid them becoming too mushy. You can also shred them and use them like any other cabbage.

Cabbage,

Cabbage is a wonderfully versatile veg. You can use it in salads, make coleslaw, put it in soups and casseroles, you can stir fry it or sauté it and you can freeze it.

Whichever way you prepare your cabbage, make sure you wash it thoroughly and dry it after blanching before you freeze it

If you have shredded it or separated the leaves allow about a 1½ minutes blanching time.

If you've cut the whole cabbage into quarters, keeping the core intact, allow about 3 minutes.

Carrots

Carrots are an easy go-to addition to many recipes as well as making lovely soup, so they are a great vegetable to have in your freezer.

Wash them and peel them is you prefer, if they are fresh from the garden or farmers market, I don't bother peeling them.

If you have diced them or cut them into strips, allow about two minutes, if you are blanching whole small carrots allow about five minutes.

Cauliflower

Make sure your cauliflower is fresh, you want to freeze crisp cauliflower to get the best out of it when it's frozen.

If you have cut your florets about 1 inch across, allow 3 minutes. Dry thoroughly and freeze on a baking sheet as individual pieces

If you like cauliflower rice, cut into small florets, wash and dry thoroughly and then rice. I like to use a food processor, but you can use a grater. I also like to rice a few cauliflowers to make the most of the prep time. Separate it into serving sized portions and freeze. It should last about 2 months.

Corn.

Corn is lovely, but it does tend to come in a glut and it's well worth preserving because it's so useful in so many recipes.

If you decide to freeze it on the cob, you need to blanch it for between 7 and 11 minutes, depending on the size of the cob.

If you are freezing kernels, allow about 4 minutes and add some salt to the water.

Greens

Spinach, kale, chard, beet greens, endive, Bok Choi (Pak Choi) arugula (rocket), any of them should take 2 to 3 minutes, if you leave them much longer they will be cooked rather than blanched.

Kohl Rabi

if you have cut it allow about a minute, if you're blanching it whole, blanch for about three minutes.

Mushrooms

If you have a sudden glut of mushrooms, you can freeze them, but it is best to prepare them first.

Slice them into quarters them, dip them into an acidic solution, for instance, a pint of water with a teaspoon of lemon juice, and leave them for five minutes. This stops them darkening.

Then steam them for between three and five minutes depending on the size and whether you have sliced them or left small mushrooms whole. Cool them quickly and drain and then pack them, leaving some space in the container, then freeze.

You can also fry them until almost cooked and then allow them to cool before packing them again, leaving some air in the container and freezing

Okra

Okra should be blanched whole for between three and four minutes.

If you want to freeze without blanching, wash it and make sure you completely dry it to avoid any condensation

Onion rings

If you love to use onions as rings, peel and cut your onions and then will only take about 15 seconds to blanch, although there is really no need to blanch onions.

You can also chop then into small pieces or freeze them whole if small or cut in half if larger.

However, onions do store well without being frozen. A whole raw onion can last for up to 3 months in the fridge. Wrap them in paper bags, not plastic. If you grow your own and want to store them, dry them properly, tie them in strings and keep in a cool, dark place for six months or more.

Peas

Peas in their pods, such as mangetout take about two minutes to blanch.

Green peas out of their pods take about a 1½ minutes and black eye peas about two minutes.

Sweet peppers

If you have cut them into strips or rings, allow about two minutes and if you have simply halved them, allow about three minutes

Not to Blanch

Most vegetables can also be frozen without being blanched, just washed, chopped if required and dried thoroughly.

It's up to you to decide what method suits you best.

Most vegetables that are frozen without blanching will not last as long in the freezer, but if you use them fairly fast and have a quick turnaround of the stock in your freezer, you might prefer to save the time in the preparation stage.

Try them and see how it suits you.

Just make sure to wash them carefully and dry really well to avoid freezer burn.

Cook before freezing

There are some foods that are better to cook and then freeze.

These include beets, pumpkins, sweet potatoes and most squash.

Some vegetables store perfectly well for long periods without freezing, such as potatoes and root vegetables, and I would only freeze these if they have been cooked first, such as potatoes prepared into fries or hash browns, or sliced unused as a topping for cottage pie, which is then frozen as your own ready meal.

Vegetables which freeze well include:

- Asparagus
- Beans – most varieties
- Beets
- Broccoli
- Cabbage (only use for cooking)
- Carrots
- Cauliflower
- Celery
- Corn
- Eggplant (Aubergine)
- Greens (Kale, mustard and turnip)
- Okra
- Parsnips
- Peas (black-eyed and green)
- Pumpkin
- Sweet potatoes
- Rutabagas and turnips
- Summer squash
- Tomatoes (stewed, only use for cooking)

Freezing Meat & Fish

Most people think of frozen food being meat or fish that is already processed, for instance, chicken nuggets, fish fingers, quarter pounders.

But you can freeze almost any type of meat or fish

Never re-freeze

The most important thing to remember, especially with meat or fish is that make absolutely sure that it hasn't been previously frozen.

Obviously if you're buying things from a freezer department, they are frozen, They stay frozen as you carry them home, you put them in the freezer and they have never been thawed and that's fine.

With other products, if they are processed, it's really important to check the packaging to see if they are suitable for freezing.

If they have been previously frozen and thawed before being putting out on the shelf, then you must not freeze them again.

The same goes for anything that you take out of the freezer.

Once you have taken raw meat or fish and cooked it into a dish, then you can freeze the meal you have prepared, but you must never refreeze any remaining ingredients that you haven't cooked.

Freezing meat is a real money saver.

Buying in bulk means that you can bring your shopping bill down quite substantially, whether that's chicken breasts, fish fillets or ground beef.

It also means that you have the meat or fish on hand when you want to prepare a meal.

But it's really important to freeze correctly for health reasons and to keep the quality of the meat.

If you have bought an excess of fresh meat or fish, you should freeze it as quickly as possible.

This is to maintain the quality of the meat.

If it freezes slowly, ice crystals can form which can make it drier or tougher when you are cooking with it.

For practical reasons, it's best to divide any large pieces of meat or fish into meal size portions, and of course do remember to label it.

You need to know the date you freeze it, what it is and what quality and cut it is.

Package the portions separately, either in freezer bags or cartons, or wrapping each piece individually in the case of things like fish fillets or chicken breasts.

Always use good quality, freezer safe food wrap.

It's best to freeze things like this in a single layer so that they will freeze evenly and without creating huge lumps, once they are frozen you can stack them to save space.

Although technically meat will last almost indefinitely in a freezer, it's recommended that you don't store it for more than a year if you want to enjoy it.

If you are freezing processed products such as bacon, sausages or sliced luncheon meats, you should really only leave it in the freezer for about two months,

Hamburgers and minced meat can be frozen for about four months.

Fresh poultry is the best choice if you need to freeze for longer, the quality of that when thawed, should last for up to a year.

When you are thawing meat or fish, put it in the fridge to thaw slowly and gently.

Do not leave it out on the counter as bacteria can form in the room temperature heat.

You should also avoid putting frozen meat in a slow cooker, the lower, slow temperature means that the meat is in the temperature danger zone for too long.

If you plan on freezing a lot of fresh meat, it can be worth investing in a vacuum sealing.

As the name suggests, these machines remove all air from the packaging which means you are not freezing air and removes the chance of contamination and freezer burn, which although leaving your meat safe to eat, can cause discolouration and poor taste.

A vacuum sealer makes it easier to freeze in the portion size you want, reducing waste when you thaw the meal

It also means that you do save a lot of space because you are only freezing the product.

Poultry

Although chicken and other poultry are one of the most commonly used meat proteins, they can also be one of the trickiest when it comes to food safety.

If you buy fresh chicken or poultry, it's very important to freeze it as soon as possible to avoid the risk of salmonella.

You shouldn't keep it in the fridge for more than two days before freezing.

Ideally, you should freeze as soon as you get it home.

Fish

Always use the freshest fish possible if you are choosing to freeze it yourself rather than buying it ready frozen. If you are buying packs of frozen fish, always read the instructions on the packaging.

Safe freezer time

Food safety advice from the US government site, says that frozen meat kept at the correct temperature and stored correctly, stays safe to eat indefinitely, but although you wouldn't starve, that doesn't mean that you'll enjoy it when you cook with it.

There are guidelines about how long you should freeze foods for if you want to keep the quality.

Processed meats such as sausages, bacon and hotdogs should be fine for up to 6 months

Ground (minced) beef, turkey, pork or lamb, keep in the freezer for 4 months.

Steak or chops, 6-8 months.

Chicken varies on how it is prepares, If you freeze a whole chicken you can store it for up to a year, separated into parts, store it for up to 9 months, but boneless chicken breasts should be used within 6 months.

Cooked meats should only be frozen for 2 to 3 months

Oily fish such as mackerel, salmon and sardines should only be frozen for up to 3 months. Other types of fish, such as cod, tuna, haddock or bass can be frozen for up to 8 months.

Thawing

After the freeze, there comes the thaw.

This is true not only of spring after winter, but using your food after getting it out the freezer.

You should never thaw food at room temperature for instance on the kitchen worktop, leaving it in the garage or basement, or anywhere else you might think of.

When you thaw food at room temperature, there is always a risk of it developing bacteria.

The safest way is to leave it in the fridge, but of course this can take some time, even a day or more, if you are thawing a larger chunk of meat.

So planning ahead is important

Of course, you can also cook it from frozen as long as you remember that the cooking process will take a lot longer, possibly twice as long.

It really is always best to try and think ahead and to take the meat or fish out of the freezer the day before you want to cook with it if you haven't allowed yourself time to thaw out your meat properly before turning it into meal there are some cooking methods that are better than others.

Chicken

Rather than trying to grill or sauté frozen chicken, try simmering in a sauce or baking and allow it to cook for about twice as long as you would with fresh or fully thawed pieces. Make sure you allow them to cook all the way through, rather than having a chilled centre where bacteria can survive.

Steak

If you have a sudden requirement for a steak and it's still in the freezer, leave it in its packaging and put it under cold water.

Once you can remove the packaging, Sauté it in a hot pan for about three minutes and then put it in the oven for a further 15 minutes, making sure that it is heated all the way through.

Pork

Pork can be cooked from frozen as long as you allow it cook for twice as long as normal and at a higher temperature.

You can cook it in the oven on the grill or even in a pan or casserole.

Things to avoid

Never put frozen meat into a slow cooker.

The fact that it is at a lower temperature for quite a long time means that bacteria can grow, which is dangerous.

So always make sure that you have fully thawed any meat before putting it in the slow cooker unless you want a side of salmonella with your casserole.

The general guide is to think ahead.

Always take meat or fish out of the freezer the night before you want to cook with it and leave it in the fridge to thaw slowly and safely.

Of course, the exception to this is when you are cooking frozen processed foods such as those chicken nuggets, fish fingers or burgers or cottage pies.

In this case, follow the instructions on the packaging.

Many of them are designed to be cooked from frozen.

Freezing herbs.

Herbs are the magic ingredient in many dishes.

They can lift your cooking from ordinary to gourmet.

The flavour that herbs give, have to be experienced to really understand what a difference simply adding a few leaves can make to your cooking.

Mostly we think of herbs as dried in little pots that come from the supermarket, although many supermarkets are now selling pots or packets of live herbs, which are rather like buying a bunch of flowers.

The problem is they don't last very long, especially if they are already cut, and the normal scenario is you pick a few of the leaves, use them in a recipe that you bought them for and then the rest just wilt and die.

Of course, really the best way to have your herbs is to grow your own fresh, which is surprisingly easy, even on a windowsill.

But once you have this wonderful selection of herbs whether they are fresh from the supermarket or even fresher from your windowsill gardening what do you do with them?

If you have them actually growing, it's easy to pick the leaves you need, use them, and then the plant remains, and you can pick again the next time you need them for a recipe.

But what happens out of season?

Although fresh herbs are wonderful, you can still enjoy the herbs whether you grow them or buy them in the supermarket, you can use them all year with a number of easy techniques.

Of course you can dry your own herbs, and that is quite easy, but you can also freeze them, which makes them even easier to use.

The best herbs for freezing are.
- Basil,
- Chervil
- Cilantro (coriander)
- Chives
- Dill.
- Lemon balm.
- Lemon verbena

- Lovage
- Mint
- Oregano
- Parsley
- Rosemary.
- Sage.
- Savoury
- Sorrell
- Sweet cicely
- Sweet Marjoram
- Tarragon
- Thyme

Some of them, such as basil, will discolour, but the flavour remains.

When you are working with herbs, you are working with the essential oils, that's why when you squeeze a leaf between your fingers, as you crush the leaf you release the oils and get the scent of the mint or thyme.

If you are growing your own herbs in the garden, and you want to collect some for preserving, early morning is the best time before the sun gets too hot.

And if you are growing your own herbs, you may as well make sure you are getting the best from them.

When you freeze herbs, you are preserving these essential oils.

There is no need to blanch them, just rinse them, take the leaves from the stems, especially with woody stems, and then dry them on a flat tray.

Once they dry you can simply gather the leaves.

Put them in a bag and freeze them.

They will freeze in a clump, but you can simply cut off the amount you want and add it to your casseroles or soups or sauces as you are cooking.

You can also freeze the leaves on a flat tray so that they freeze individually as you would with berries.

Then, once they are frozen and you put them in their storage bags or boxes, and you can pick out individual leaves as you need them.

You can also make your own herb oil by blending the herbs with oil into a paste.

You can either use this to create individual herbal pastes such as basil, or you can make your own blends with your own preferred herbs.

If you are using this method, it's best to use small containers, such as an ice cube tray or very small freezer safe containers.

Then you can simply take one or possibly two flavour bombs to use in your recipe.

You can also create your own pesto and freeze that.

And of course, if you prefer, you can take the leaves, cut them into small pieces, cover them in water in small containers and freeze that.

The method you choose is up to you and it really depends on the type of cooking that you like to do.

Try different things out and see which you prefer.

Once you have frozen your herbs, they can stay fresh in the freezer for up to a year and freezing is a surprisingly good way of retaining the flavour rather than drying them. In fact, the taste is the same as when they are fresh, although they might not look as pretty if you want to put them on your salad.

I love to have an easy selection of flavour bombs ready to go straight from the freezer.

Garlic Warning

If you are thinking of preserving garlic, take great care with how you do it. Garlic in oil can produce the deadly toxin botulism, which although it is popular for getting rid of wrinkles (botox) it is certainly not something to mess with unless you know exactly what you are doing.

The problem occurs when you store garlic without a supply of oxygen, and of course preserving it in oil does exactly that.

Raw garlic, garlic cooked in oil or preserved in vinegar is safe. Garlic in oil and then frozen in safe in theory, but it depends on how it was prepared and how long it was left at room temperature.

I would recommend using commercially prepared garlic in oil if you have to. Better safe than sorry.

What else can you freeze.

We all know the basics that you can freeze.

Garden peas, chicken pieces, pizzas, or ice cream.

You know you can freeze them because they come from the freezer department in the food stores.

But there are all sorts of foods that you can freeze and some of them are a bit unexpected.

And we've had a look at the fruit and veg, the meat and the herbs that are suitable for freezing, but your freezer can take some unexpected items as well

Cakes.

Yes, you can freeze cakes.

Not only cakes but muffins or cookies, flapjacks and all sorts of baked goods.

This is great if you like cake, but you don't want to eat it all the time.

Many people avoid having cake in house because they either eat it all and wish they hadn't, or don't eat it all and put it out for the birds once it's gone stale.

But knowing that you can freeze this treat, opens up a whole new world.

Just wrap the slices or individual cupcakes, cookies, muffins or flapjacks in food wrap or clingfilm and put them in the freezer.

Then when you fancy a treat. you can take them out and either defrost them in the microwave or leave them to defrost naturally.

Of course, you can always have them frozen with some ice cream or yoghurt.

Your very own cookies and cream.

Bread

A lot of the freshly baked bread that you get in supermarkets is actually delivered as frozen dough to the store.

So of course, you can freeze dough or bread.

If you don't get through much bread and you find that you normally throw out at least half a loaf, being able to freeze it can save you a lot of waste.

When you buy a fresh loaf, separate it into individual servings, wrap them in food wrap and put them in the freezer.

That means that when you want your toast, you can take out two or four slices and put them straight in the toaster. Many toasters now have a toast from frozen button, so you don't even have to defrost it.

If you do bake your own bread, you can put the dough in the freezer to be taken out when you want to bake it and still enjoy freshly baked bread without having to do all the preparation each time.

Of course, you can also buy part baked rolls in food stores.

And it's not just bread.

You can freeze unbaked scones as well.

Just make the dough, separate it into the portions that you want and freeze them wrapped in food wrap.

Then, when you fancy a fresh scone, take the dough from the freezer and put in the oven.

Milk.

Milk can be frozen and stored for months,

I do it all the time.

It's very useful if you want to bulk buy rather than stepping out for fresh milk every few days.

If you are decanting it into other containers, do make sure that there is some space so that the milk can expand, otherwise it might burst.

You can freeze milk for about three months.

Take it out the night before you need it and leave it to defrost slowly in the fridge.

I find I need to shake the bottle a bit the next morning, and for a few hours I do have iced milk, but that's fine in your morning coffee if you need to cool it down quickly.

Cheese.

Milk isn't the only dairy item that you can freeze.

Cheese freezes very well.

If you find that you have leftover pieces of cheese, rather that throwing them away, simply put them all in a tub that you keep in the freezer.

Then you can remove them and add chunks to a sauce that you are cooking.

If you want to be able to use it as a topping or in a sandwich, it's best to grate it before freezing it.

As long as you keep it in an airtight container or squeeze the air out of the bag you store it in, it won't clump together.

If you find yourself in a rush in the morning, you can take some, grated cheese out of the freezer and make a sandwich and it will have defrosted by lunchtime.

It's also perfect for topping a dish of pasta or a pizza.

You can also freeze cottage cheese and whipped cream, and it's perfectly all right to freeze butter or margarine, as long as you only leave it frozen for about three months.

Berries.

The course you probably know that you can freeze berries, because you can buy bags of them from the freezer cabinet.

But that doesn't mean you can't freeze your own berries and make the most of seasonal glut where you can either harvest lots of your own from the garden or buy them at very reasonable prices in the grocery store.

This saves the problem of berries going off.

When you buy fresh berries in stores or when your harvests are coming in all at the same time, you can find yourself with a large amount of berries, far more than you can really eat at one time, especially as they don't stay fresh for very long and there's a limit to just how many fruit pies or jars of jam you want to make.

When you're preparing your berries for freezing just wash them in a colander, pat them dry and remove any damaged or unripe berries and pieces of stem.

You can freeze them as individual varieties or make up your own berry mix.

When you are freezing them, put them in a freezer bag in a single layer and lie it flat, so that when they freeze, they are not in one big clump.

That makes it much easier to open and take a few out to add to your smoothie, your juice, your yoghurt or even into porridge.

And while you're freezing berries try freezing grapes.

I love frozen grapes and they make a wonderful alternative to ice cubes.

You'll surprise your friends if you serve frozen grapes with some nice cheese at the end of dinner. Very gourmet.

When you put them in a drink instead of an ice cube, they're not going to dilute your drink.

And if you just eat them as grapes, they're like miniature grape flavoured lollies without the additional sugar.

Pasta

Obviously, you don't need to freeze dry pasta because it's dried and it lasts.

But once you have cooked pasta, then freezing it is a great time saver, especially when you freeze it as a complete meal with the sauce.

If you're cooking a pasta meal, try and leave your pasta a little al dente, so that when you reheat it, it still retains some texture.

It saves a lot of money if you make your pasta dishes in a big batch, because you're saving on the electricity or gas you use and you can buy the items in bulk, such as the tomato sauce, any vegetables and herbs without wasting any of it.

You also save a lot of time, because it means you can have your own healthier ready meals in the freezer that you can just take out and reheat in the microwave.

If I want to add a cheese topping to a tomato pasta dish, I add that when I'm reheating it, but I make cheesy pastas as a finished dish.

When you are freezing them as your own ready meals, remember not to use foil trays if you want to microwave them.

Nuts

Although nuts seem like something you can keep in a container, they can go bad very quickly because of their high oil content.

So, if you buy big packets of nuts and you don't think you're going to get through them all, put them in a sealed bag and freeze them.

When you do need to use them, simply take the amount you need out of the freezer and they should thaw in about an hour or two at room temperature.

This means that you can take advantage of the savings of buying large quantities of nuts.

Frozen they should last at least six months and up to 12 months.

Chocolate.

If chocolate lasts more than a couple of days for you, you can freeze it.

I know, when does chocolate last?

But you might have found a really good deal, and stocked up

The trick to freezing chocolate is to do it gradually.

Wrap it up tightly in a freezer bag and then put it in the fridge for several hours before you move it into the freezer.

And then do this in reverse when you want to bring it out.

If you can possibly restrain yourself, chocolate can stay in the freezer for about six months

Gin

And vodka and other alcohol.

Alcohol won't actually freeze in a domestic freezer, it doesn't get cold enough, but why would you want to put a bottle of gin or vodka in the freezer anyway?

Gin is best served cold. It makes the taste a little more gentle and makes it easier to drink. You should always keep your gin in the fridge rather than a cupboard according to some experts, as it doesn't freeze because of the percentage of alcohol, it's also safe to put in the freezer – alongside the ice cubes of course.

Its quite common to find bottles of vodka in a freezer as well. Again, it won't actually freeze, but it does become a little thicker and although that doesn't mean it becomes a syrup, apparently it gives it a richer taste. Of course, if you have a good vodka, full of flavours, you might want to keep it the way the distillery intended.

The very way that a cold climate affects the taste of gin and vodka, is the same reason that you shouldn't put whisky, rum or brandy in the freezer, you will dull the flavour, so room temperature is best for them.

Beer and wine have lower alcohol contents than a bottle of spirits, so they will freeze, although not a solid as water. That's why you can make wine ice cubes for using in recipes.

If you really need a cool beer or a glass of chilled wine, you can pop them in the freezer but only for about 15 to 30 minutes, depending on your preference.

Don't leave them for much longer or store them in the freezer, the bottles are not designed for freezer use and they could burst and them you'll have pieces of glass all over your freezer, definitely not a good idea.

Freeze-Ahead Meals and Sauces

This is where knowing how to make the best use of your freezer really comes into its own.

Using the freezer as your own convenience store.

Have you ever wished you could fill your freezer with meals that are already prepared and ready to heat and eat? Oh, wait a minute, they are called TV dinners.

But of course, lots of them come with added salt, sugar and fats you can't identify.

And sometimes they're not even that tasty or satisfying either.

Let's be honest, sometimes the best you can say about them is that they are food – well sort of food!

But they are convenient.

There are times when you really can't face preparing a meal at the end of a long day and you reach for something that will just fill the gap, then often wished you hadn't.

The answer is to batch cook.

As a qualified nutritionist, I like to know exactly what I'm eating.

I'm also a strong believer in the idea that good food is good medicine, you literally are what you eat.

This means that I like to prepare my own meals from fresh ingredients.

But although I am very interested in what I eat and the nutritional value of what I eat, I'm not actually keen on spending a lot of time in the kitchen preparing the meals, so I tend to batch cook.

I will gather my fresh vegetables and herbs, either from the garden or from farm shops or supermarkets and spend the day preparing them, cooking them, creating meals and freezing them.

This means that I always have a supply of my own ready meals, so I have the convenience of meals that I can just take out of the freezer and put in the microwave if I'm short of time, but I know what I'm eating and I know exactly what has gone into it.

This makes the freezer an invaluable tool for me.

Obviously, as a vegetarian, all of my meals are based around vegetables, but you can follow exactly the same idea of batch cooking and creating your own supply of ready meals with meat and fish if you're not vegetarian.

You can save a lot of money and time when you batch cook and freeze your own meals.

In effect, you are creating your own ready meals without the hassle and cost of filling up a trolly at the store.

And you can be sure that you are creating meals that you will like, that have the ingredients that you want, that can be healthier and- of course - can save you a lot of money.

You can take advantage of buying in season, which means that the fruit and veg are more available, cost less, are fresher and will have far fewer food miles.

That's better for you, better for your wallet, better for the local farmers and better for the environment

So make the change and cook up healthy, tasty meals that you and the family enjoy, and really get the most out of your freezer.

You will know what you are eating and exactly what has gone into the meal.

You can choose to use organic, home grown, slow grown, healthy fats, natural sugars, less salt – whatever your preference.

You can choose to make a great choice of vegetarian or vegan meals if that's your choice, rather than loading up on carbs, lots of ready meals without meat are full of carbs.

And when you have finished cooking the delicious meals, you can put them into the portion sizes you will use and freeze them.

Remembering to label them of course.

And if you want to use your microwave, remember not to use foil trays.

You have created your own convenience store.

Ready meals waiting to be taken out and re-heated at the end of a long, tiring day.

You can do the same with sauces and soups as well.

Instead of reaching for a jar of sauce to make pasta, take your own home-made sauce out of the freezer.

There are so many benefits to cooking from scratch.

- You know where your food is from.
- You know what's in it.
- You can choose the flavours and the amount of flavour or spice that you enjoy.
- You can have the servings in the sizes that suit you and your family.
- You're helping to protect the environment – no un-necessary throw away packaging, fewer food miles
- You can save a lot of money.

That last one can make a really big difference to your budget.

Why spend money you don't have to?

Preparing to cook

Preparing your own ready meals does take some planning and some time.

It is important to plan what meals you are going to prepare before you start, if you want to get the best out of your batch cooking session.

Then you can make your shopping list and go and gather the ingredients you will need.

Of course, you can also do it the other way around.

See what is in season, what you have just picked in the garden or what is on offer in store and plan your recipes around that.

That is the real money saver.

One of the easiest types of meals to do as a freeze-ahead meal is a casserole.

A casserole is a term that can be used to cover almost any type of one pot cooking.

I like to use my trusty cast iron pot on the hob and fill the kitchen with wonderful smells, but if you want a true casserole, put it in the oven.

One pot cooking can give you vegetarian, vegan or meat meals.

It can be a sturdy winter dish, a flavourful curry, a Mexican bean chilli, a stew, a hotpot, a jambalaya – the list is almost endless.

It's an easy type of cooking.

You can use a traditional casserole pot, a slow cooker, a pressure cooker or one of the new systems of combined, one-pot cooking.

You can make is as simple or as complex as you like.

I tend to set aside a day for my batch cooking and have everything cooking at once, including a wonderful microwave pressure cooker that can produce a tasty vegetable curry from raw veggies in about 20 minutes.

The I batch them all up in freezer bags and microwave safe storage boxes, let them cool and then stock the freezer with my very own collection of ready meals.

If you want some inspiration about what kind of ready meals you can make for your freezer, take a trip to your grocery store and spend a while looking in the freezer section.

Alongside the bags of veg, chicken pieces, fish fingers and tubs of ice cream, you'll find a wide array of meals or parts of meals.

In the past, you've probably just picked out the pizzas and burgers than you always buy, without really looking at the full range and the vast choice.

Being time poor, means you just go to the same section every time.

You can get lasagne, mac and cheese or spaghetti bolognaise.

You can get curries of every type.

Pies, pasties and sausage rolls, either cooked or ready to bake.

Burgers and patties in every variety.

Stir fry, risotto and paella.

In fact, you can get almost anything you can think of if you look in the freezer section of a large food shop.

If you look in the freezer cabinet in a farm shop, you'll find a whole selection of home made goodies

And if you can buy it frozen, you can make your own and freeze it.

Which means that you can batch cook and create your own meals in an almost endless variety.

Lasagna is a very popular meal to make ahead and freeze. You will need noodles, spaghetti sauce (homemade or store bought), cheese and meat if you use it. You can also use Quorn, but I like aubergine (eggplant) in my vegetarian lasagne.

Prepare the lasagne as if you're going to eat it right away, but don't bake it now, you can put it in the oven for the final baking when you defrost it. When you have added the last cheese layer, place a cover on it and let it cool. When it has fully cooled, put it in the freezer and it will cool evenly.

If you plan to finish off any meals in the oven you can store them in aluminium containers, just remember not to put them in the microwave.

The list of possible home ready made meals is endless, limited only by what you want to eat.

Not just one pot meals either.

You can get freezer quality packaging for all sorts of batch cooking. Just check out the internet and find cartons for preparing the type of meal we think of as Sunday lunch.

Trays with 2 or three compartments to separate your meat or nut roast, potatoes and vegetables.

Trays to keep your curry and rice separate.

Trays to keep your

Whatever meals you want to eat – apart from salad, that just gets soggy – can be pre-prepared and loaded into your beautifully organised freezer to create your own, high quality, convenience food store

It doesn't just have to be a full meal.

You can also make your favourite soups.

Make a big pot of Chili and freeze it in convenient portion sizes to add to other things like rice, flatbread, tortillas or potato when you are in need of some comfort food.

Quick meals often see you reaching for a jar of pasta sauce, but it's so easy to make your own and freeze it in the portion sizes you want.

That means you know what's in it, you save a fortune, you always have it on hand and you don't end up with half a jar in the fridge before it makes its way to the bin,

Don't say you've never done that, everybody's done that!

Buy tomatoes when they are in season and at a great price. If you don't want to do the prep work on fresh tomatoes, use basic tins of chopped tomatoes or passata. Adding the rest of your ingredients will turn it from basic to tasty, the type of sauce that can cost four or five times the price of the basic tomatoes.

Prepare the sauce with your favourite ingredients. Your family will be able to taste the difference and the love.

You can add onion, basil, garlic, oregano, pepper or chilli, sugar or go sugar free, salt and pepper. You can get adventurous and add whatever ingredient you would like to try. Just search the internet and find some recipes you'd like to experiment with.

Creamy pasta sauces don't freeze as well as tomato ones, and if I want to add cheese or yoghurt, I prefer to add it fresh once I have defrosted the sauce for cooking.

In fact, just experiment with batch cooking.

It might seem odd and even a little time consuming when you first think about it.

But once you've been able to reach into your freezer and take out a tasty ratatouille when you get home instead of making a cheese sandwich , once you've been able to enjoy a thick and satisfying home made soup in minutes or had a fresh lasagne on the table in the time it takes you to have a shower after work, you'll be hooked.

Ice cube trays

We all got ice cube trays.

Most freezers come with at least one and we all know what they are for.

You put water in it and make ice cubes.

But there's so much more you can do and some of these little trays can almost be the most useful thing in your freezer, so here are some ideas.

Ice cubes of course. It's always useful to have some ice cubes. Why lug bags back from the store when you only want a few cubes for your summer squash?

Yes, they can go in your gin and tonic, but they are also great if you want crushed ice drinks in a hot summer or you want to add some extra cool to your smoothie.

So it's always worth having a tray or two of ice cubes if you have space.

But you can do so much more

About ice cube trays.

I find that silicon trays are the easiest to use.

Sometimes the more rigid trays make it so difficult to get the contents out that you don't bother. But a good silicon tray will simply pop an individual cube out when you need it.

You can find them in all sorts of fancy shapes as well, which is fun.

You can find flowers and hearts, smiley faces and shark fins, stars and snowflakes. In fact, silicon is so mouldable that you can find almost anything.

Ice cube trays are one of the more reasonably priced pieces of kitchen equipment, so it's worth investing in good quality trays that will last and that you will use rather than abandon in frustration.

And they really are useful pieces of equipment.

If you do have more rigid trays, I find it much easier if I take it out of the freezer and let it sit on the bench for about one minute rather than all the trouble of running under water and bashing on the edge of the sink, only to find that eventually the whole tray of cubes drop out.

Once it has been sitting for 30-60 seconds, you can normally pry a single cube out easily by slipping a knife down one edge – carefully. Then you can pop the rest of the tray back in the freezer.

You can get ice cube trays with lids if you would like to stack them, but of course, once they are frozen, they stack easily enough anyway.

Another advantage of a lid is that it will help to keep odours in or out of your cubes and it will keep your cubes clean, you don't want to have your drink with crumbs of pastry.

Another way of storing your cubes is to freeze whatever it is you want to freeze, then remove them all from the tray. Wrap them individually in freezer quality food wrap and store them in a box in the freezer. Then it's easy enough to just pick one out when needed.

Once they're wrapped in food wrap they won't stick together, but remember to label the box.

Lemon cubes

Talking of the gin and tonic – we were, honestly.

When you buy lemons, limes or oranges, quite often you'll use the first few and then the others will just sit around going hard and end up in the bin. So why not juice all of them as soon as you get them home, when they're still beautiful and fresh?

Then you can freeze the juice in ice cube trays. After that, it's a simple matter of popping one out when you want to make a honey and lemon hot drink, or a gin and tonic or you want to thaw some lemon or lime out to put in a recipe. It means you will never waste those beautiful fruit again.

Pesto

If you've made pesto and have some left over, put it in an ice cube tray. Then you have simple individual blocks to use when needed.

Flavour bomb

A recipe always needs some flavour, so when you have some leftover broth or stock, turn it into your own flavour bomb.

Ginger

And when you are using some ginger, rather than just using the amount you want, and often leaving the rest to go to waste, just grate the whole piece and put the extras into a tray.

Herbs

Fresh herbs are one of the most wasted ingredients in the kitchen. You buy the bunch from the store, take them home and use a handful for that special recipe, then put the rest in the fridge where they quickly go off and make the trip to the bin.

But you can save yourself from sad looking herbs.

They are simple to store in ice cube trays.

Just wash them, chop them, fill up your ice cube tray, add some water, making sure the herbs are covered, and freeze.

You can also cover them with oil or stock and freeze them. Then you can simply pop one out later on to add to a soup or pasta, a stew or casserole.

Along the same lines, why not make up a strong chili mix. Again, simply pour it into the ice cube tray for easy individual shots. Then, when you need a chili bomb to spice up your recipe, pop it out of the tray and into the pot.

Leftovers

You can freeze almost any leftover ingredients.

Quite often a recipe will call for a relatively small amount of a special item, but you can only buy it in much bigger amounts.

So you make up the recipe and then the extra sits in the fridge, and then you throw it out.

But many of these ingredients can be frozen. So next time you have extra things like cream, coconut milk, full fat milk or yoghurt, if you're not going to use them straight away, simply freeze them.

Iced Coffee

If you like iced coffee, you can also do this in an ice cube tray.

Simply make up some coffee, pour it into the tray once it's cooled, and freeze. Then you can add it to a glass of cold milk or water, or even a mug of coffee and add the ice and more coffee at the same time.

And if you're always in a rush as you make your coffee, you can make milk cubes. Then you can add your milk and cool your coffee in one shot.

Fruit

If you like putting fruit into your drinks or deserts, pop some smaller berries into the individual trays, top up with water and voilà, fruity ice cubes.

You can use things like chopped strawberries, raspberries, blackberries, blueberries or pomegranate seeds.

Talking of leftovers from recipes, it's really annoying when you use some wine and have half a bottle left that you don't drink – ok, that's doesn't happen very often!

But if it does, it's easy to forget to use it, so it stays in the cupboard or the fridge until it's really too late to use it.

Don't waste it - freeze it.

Then you can simply add however many cubes of wine you would like to a recipe without wasting another bottle.

Onions

Talking of adding flavour to a recipe, next time you caramelise onions, do some extra and then after you've used the amount you need for that recipe, you can freeze the extra and save yourself some time in chopping onions for the next recipe.

If you roast some garlic, you can mash it and fill the trays.

But do be extremely careful if you are planning on storing garlic in oil in any form. It is safe in the freezer for a couple of months, in the fridge for a couple of days and out on the bench at room temperature – not at all. The reaction can cause the toxin botulinum to develop and you can't tell from smell, look or taste.

So if you are going to store garlic in oil, freeze it straight away and use it immediately from frozen.

Eggs

You can freeze eggs.

Yes, really, and they taste just the same as they did when you thaw them again, ready to use in any way that you would normally use an egg, although the white and yolk don't separate that well.

They freeze very well and last a long time and they are one of the foods that are as good once a thawed as when they were fresh.

You can also freeze egg whites and yolks separately.

So if you have recipes that involve separating eggs, do it in advance.

If you have large ice cube trays and small eggs, just crack each one into each cubicle and freeze.

Or you can beat the eggs first and freeze them in full or half egg servings.

Summer drinks

If you like the idea of using flowers in your drinks - and there are a lot of beautiful edible flowers around - simply slip the petals into the tray, fill up with water and let it freeze for the prettiest ice cubes you've ever seen.

Pick some lavender, pansies or hibiscus flowers.

Perfect for a summer party

And of course, you can freeze cubes of fruit juice to add a hint of flavour to still or sparkling water rather than buying expensive and artificially sweet, flavoured water.

Cookie Dough

You fancy a cookie, but you have to make a whole batch and then temptation sets in. Sound familiar?

There's a perfect answer.

Marianne Duvall

Mix up a batch of cookie dough, freeze in separate portions in an ice cube tray, then next time you fancy a cookie you can just pop one out and cook it.

Ok – pop two out.

Yoghurt

I love freezing little treats of yoghurt, filled with fruit, raisins, nuts, seeds or even granola. They make perfect, bite sized treats.

Vacuum Sealers

I've mentioned using a vacuum sealer a few times in the previous pages, and they can be extremely useful machines if you plan on making the best use of your freezer, but it's not the find a kitchen equipment at the top of everyone's list.

You can go to the electrical or department store and find an almost endless supply of exciting gadgets for the kitchen.

From coffee makers to fancy kettles, juicers, smoothie makers and powerful blenders. You can find, electric knives, pie makers, slow cookers, multi cookers, air-fryers and pressure cookers, stand mixers, hand mixers and stick mixers, the list is almost endless – and I have to admit, I've got quite a few of them.

But how often do you see a food vacuum sealer?

Not very often.

But air is the enemy when you want to store food, either in the cupboard or in the freezer.

The oxygen changes the taste, the texture the colour and the smell of food, it also evaporates the natural moisture, causing food to dry out.

The reaction with air causes freezer burn in the freezer, it means that your store cupboard foods don't last as long as you like and that oils in nuts and other foods oxidise and deteriorate.

In other words, food doesn't last as long as it could when air gets to it.

So getting the air out of your food is a good idea.

We always do this by resealing packaging, pushing as much air out as possible when using sealable bags and wrapping food tightly before storing it, but although that helps, none of it can remove the air completely.

That's where vacuum sealers come in.

You can find containers that are designed for vacuum sealing. They have special lids that fit the pump that is designed for them. They have their uses, but they can be bulky, you have to have the pump – so don't lose it – and they have to be re-vacuumed every time you open them is you use them to store bulk items such as breakfast cereal or fresh items like salad leaves.

A vacuum sealer machine works by sucking the air out of the bag you have stored your food in.

You can see examples of this if you look in the meat, fish or cheese sections of the food store. The strong, clear wrap is tight to the piece of salmon, the steak or the cheese block or the cucumber.

Vacuum sealing is popular in professional kitchens as well as in the home because it means that food can be stored safely for much longer, up to five times longer for some types of food.

Beef and poultry can be kept in the freezer for up to 3 years instead of the normal 6 months, although 2 years is a better guide.

The storage time for fish can also be increased from 6 months to 2 years.

Stews, sauces or soup can be frozen for up to 2 years instead of 3 or 4 months and vegetables can remain freshly frozen for 2 or 3 years instead of 6-8 months.

Another benefit when you are preparing food for the freezer, is the amount of space you save. You are only freezing the food, there is very little packaging, and of course, no air.

If you visit the local fish market and buy fish straight off the boats, or you go to a local farm shop and stock up with different joints of meat, the fact that you can come home and package them for long term storage in the freezer, means that you can buy a larger amount and make the trip worthwhile.

There are a number of different vacuum seal machines available, from large and expensive pieces of equipment that are suitable for professional kitchens, to smaller and much simpler machines designed to fit the small, modern kitchen.

Obviously, you also have a range of features and prices to choose from as well.

Start by asking yourself some questions about what you want from the machine.

How much are you willing to invest in the machine?

How much space do you have to store the machine?

Are you going to store dry or moist food – or both?

How often do you think you'll use the machine?

Do you want to be able to vacuum seal containers as well as bags?

You might use it regularly for leftovers and batch cooking, or you might use it seasonally when you have a harvest glut, while certain fruit and veggies are in season and therefore available at a much lower price.

If you're going to use it regularly, it needs to be easy to reach for and easy to get the bags or film you need.

If you're going to use it seasonally, you can get it out of storage, get your bags or rolls sorted and ordered in time for a preserving spree.

As with any piece of equipment, a budget model that doesn't have the features you need is a waste of time and money, but at the other end of the scale a top level machine that will help you run a professional kitchen is also a waste of money and probably space, if you use it once a year for a relatively small amount of food.

For a regular user, on board bag roll storage is a useful feature. You just place the roll of bags in the machine, which means you always use the right size because they are custom cut each time. The rolls also work out a little cheaper than pre-cut bags, so you save money both ways.

Some machines will take bigger and wider bags than others, something to consider rather than rushing to impulse buy. I would never do that! You might disagree if you checked my cupboards.

You can get small, compact vacuum sealers, but they are limited in their usefulness and features.

There are a number of choices to make when you are deciding on a machine.

Does it have manual or automatic sealing, and what does it mean by automatic? How many buttons do you have to use, if any? If you have dexterity problems that might be important for you.

Does it have a pulse mode? If you plan on storing delicate foods such as bread, salad leaves, delicate fruit or crisps and chips, you will need to be able to draw the air out slowly in short pulses so that you don't crush the contents.

Some machines will also vacuum seal storage containers which has be opened and resealed. The lids have a valve that the machine can be connected to.

Once you begin to look at the range of machines, you will quickly see how many different things they can be used for, and the versatility of often the difference between it becoming a well-used piece of kitchen equipment and another machine in the back of the cupboard.

So read some reviews, decide what you will use it for and how often you will use it.

Check the size, the features, the availability and cost of the bags or storage rolls you will need for the machine, and then go for the one that will suit you.

A freezer and vacuum sealer go together like hot chocolate and marshmallows.

and finally ....

I hope this has given you a better idea of just how useful a freezer can be.

It is so much more than just a cupboard in the corner or the extra bit that comes attached to the fridge.

It's so much more than a convenient place to store a couple of pizzas and ready meals from the corner shop.

Used properly, a well stocked freezer can save you time and lots of money.

It can give you convenient but nutritional and tasty food that you will actually enjoy eating.

It will mean you can keep control of your health and your weight by knowing what you are eating.

It will stop food waste, lower the amount of packaging you throw out, help you reduce your food miles and support local growers.

It means that if you do grow your own, you can also store and save your own.

It can help you keep your food fresh, safe, healthy and tasty.

Your leftovers can become new, tasty meals for later instead of bin fodder.

You won't have to worry about going to the food store all the time, so you will save time as well as money.

You can stock up on multi-buy offers or special deals when you see them.

And you can save money by buying in bulk. The large bags of nuts are much more economical that the small ones, but they don't last very long on the shelf. Putting them in the freezer means that you can take advantage of the saving.

So by now you should see that having and using a freezer for more than pizza and ice cream is a very good idea.

Try and find space for a larger freezer. A taller fridge freezer with a usable freezer section if floor space is at a premium. But if you can find the space, a tall, stand alone machine will soon pay you back for your investment.

Embrace your new frozen life style.

About the Author

Marianne Duvall's passion in life is showing people how to make it easy to live a healthier life through nutrition and fitness – making small changes in everyday life that can make big changes in health and wellbeing.

She has studied how to rebalance modern life to allow space for good nutrition and activity as part of everyday life rather than an expensive and time consuming extra.

She believes that healthy living should be how we live, part of everyday life rather than an afterthought. Something so natural that we don't even think about it, we just do it.

She is a qualified nutritionist and has developed her ideas over the years while working with those living with chronic illnesses such as M.E./CFS, fibromyalgia or diabetes, developing plans that help people live successfully with these illnesses.

Her motto is 'Live Life'

Printed in Great Britain
by Amazon

62453472R00068